YOU S
HAVE ...ME
TO SAVE
YOURSELF

!!!

Printed in the United Kingdom

First Printing, 2017

ISBN 978-0-9957746-0-5

Sane Press
26 Bloomsbury Street
London
WC1B 3QJ

www.sanepress.com

Dedicated to my **very patient** wife.

Surely the whole world needs the remote controls to be aligned? Not just with each other, but with the edge of the sofa, the corner of the coffee table and the picture on the wall – bliss. Apparently most people aren't upset if a salad doesn't have an equal balance of colours or when there is "too much" space between the letter F and A in a shop sign. Designers do. So if you are contemplating sharing a confined space with one of these strange creative folk I suggest you read this book and read it quick.

If you've ever lived with a designer you will understand that they are like schizophrenic chihuahuas on ecstasy. Their strange quirks and weird habits make them squirm and jiggle with creative excitement – yet normal people will never understand these quirks. This book is designed to help you gain a small if scarily bonkers view into the psyche of the average designer.

COLOUR IS VERY IMPORTANT

Everything has to be exactly the right colour, not close – exact! A chair can't just be green; it has to be the perfect shade of green. You may say 'they're all fucking green!' but we'll argue the toss about this for hours if necessary.

ICE WHITE
192c
SNOW WHITE
193c
SUGAR WHITE
194c
LILY WHITE
195c
ANGEL WHITE
196c
PURE WHITE
197c
WHITE WHITE
198c
MIGHTY WHITE
199c
PRIEST WHITE
200c

OBSESSED WITH ORDER

Whether it's colour coded, size, texture, alphabetised – it doesn't matter; If we can put it in order then it's like Christmas has come early.

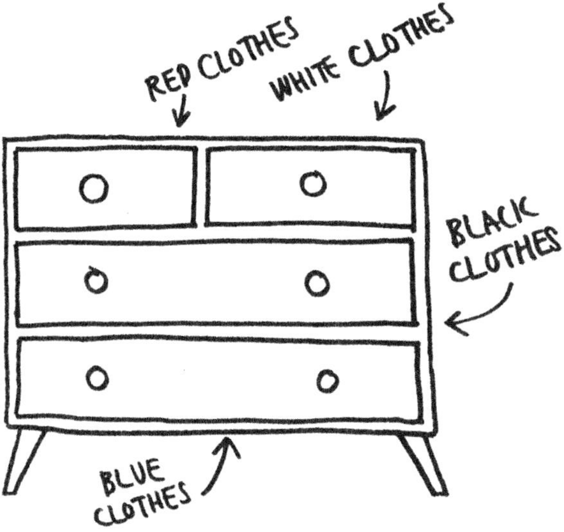
RED CLOTHES
WHITE CLOTHES
BLACK CLOTHES
BLUE CLOTHES

COOKING & CHOPPING

Everything has to be exactly right. 'Sliced thinly' for a designer means exactly half a human hair in width, 5mm deep; "Hang on my dear let me just grab a ruler…"

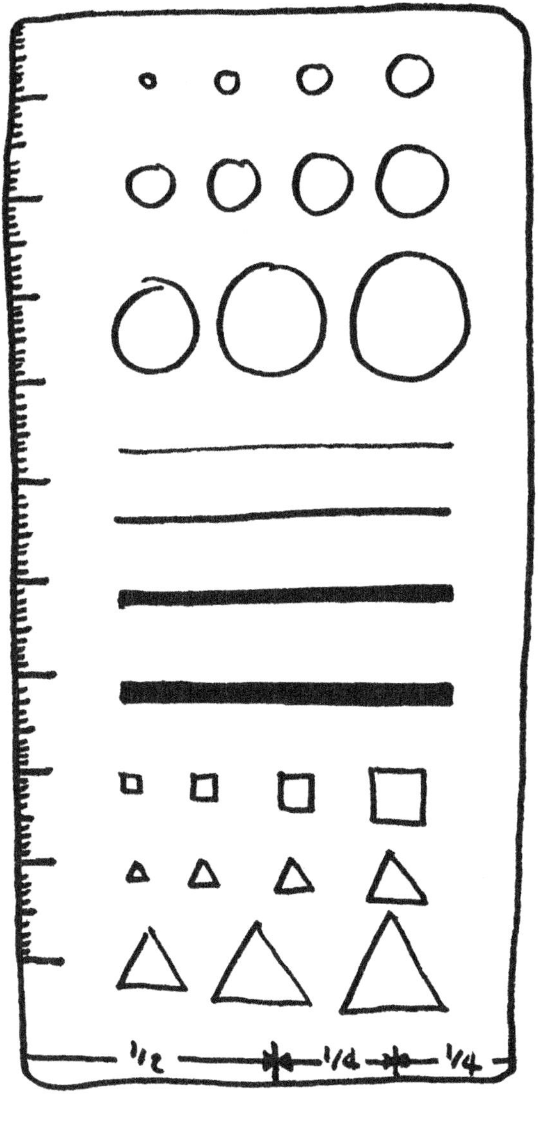
1/2
1/4
1/4

COOKING & RECIPES

Most of the world doesn't stick exactly one hundred percent to a recipe. Designer: NO. 250g flour EXACTLY, 1 medium sized onion (we will compare all onions in the world until we find the medium one).

We hate recipes with quantities like a 'pinch' or a 'dash'. Even more infuriating to our exact nature is 'some salt and pepper'. 'Some'? 'Some'??? What kind of non-measurement is that! We will lose sleep over such airy-fairy recipes.

250gm

251gm

500ml

502ml

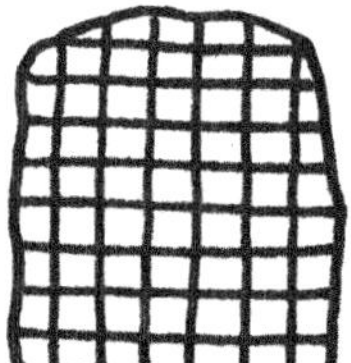

5mm

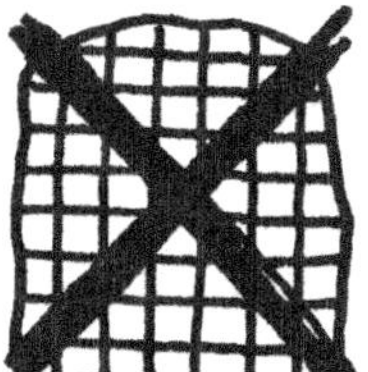

4mm

COOKING & COLOUR

When we prepare food it has to have a mix of colours. We will add extra ingredients of certain colours if a dish looks a bit too “similar” or “boring”.

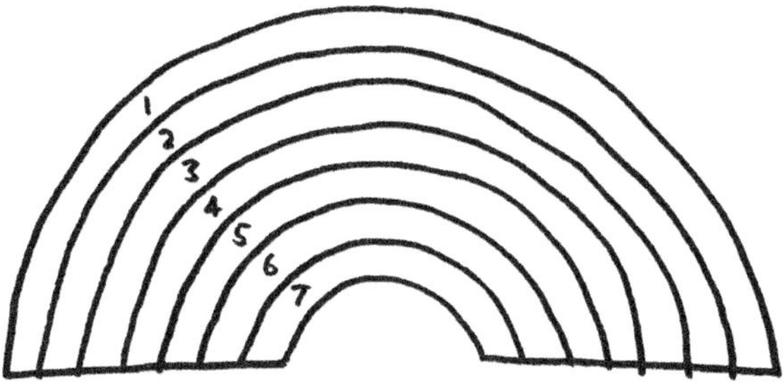

1 RED
2 YELLOW
3 PINK
4 GREEN
5 PURPLE
6 ORANGE
7 BLUE

ATTRACTED TO COOL

Designers are a natural magnet for cool. Whether it's clothes, a way to comb our hair or the latest beard and barista espresso bar. We are drawn to cool like a moth to a flame. It also works the opposite way, in that uncool repels us.

COOL
SIMON COWELL

WE COLLECT ANYTHING

We will find things on the street or tear them out of magazines. It could be anything and to most people will seem like crap. Just accept that we will have a box hidden under the bed – not full of porn but of letter A's and patterns.

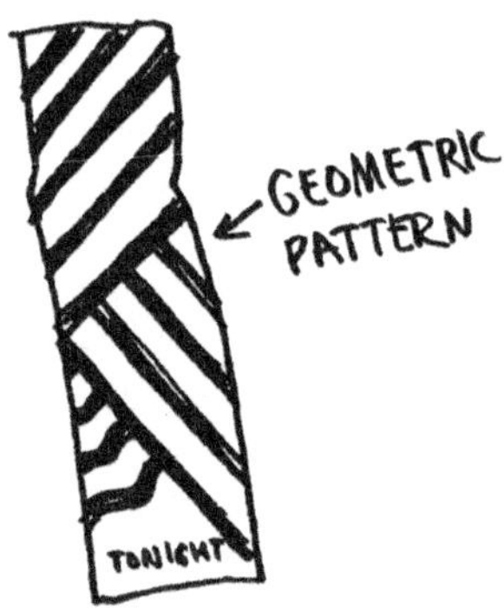

USE AS LOGO
AN
NICE PRINT
TICKET
&
HAND-DRAWN (NICE!!)
ARE
AWESOME FONT
PAPER CLIP HEART?
COOL LOGO
EYE ICON

FACIAL HAIR

Mainly the male design community, thankfully, but the affinity with facial hair of any kind is stronger than a mother and child bond!

SCALPELS AT THE READY

We use these instead of scissors. It’s slightly sinister especially as most designers have roughly twenty-nine of them ‘just in case’.

EVERYTHING NEEDS TO MATCH

Things have to match. All the same plates, cups of the same colour. This is why, ideally, our homes would be completely white – so that everything matches.

EVERYTHING NEEDS TO MATCH

Things have to match. All the same plates, cups of the same colour. This is why, ideally, our homes would be completely white – so that everything matches.

SINGLE SPEED BIKES

Normal people get excited by how many gears their bike has; designers enjoy as few as possible.

DON'T ASK FOR FAVOURS

We hate designing for friends, so please don't ask – you kill our creative skills, every time we design for friends a designer loses their wings!

IOU

IKEA SELF-ASSEMBLY

It's like an ancient language engrained deep in our DNA – designers just know how to read IKEA instructions and build even the most complex wardrobe.

WE ALWAYS FREELANCE

This is what others would call 'working two jobs', but designers do it out of fun. No, really – we actually enjoy working all the time on design, even when we get home from working on design all day.

I AM A DESIGNER
Call me!!!

WE LIKE BOOKS WITHOUT WORDS

We love 'design' books. These are normally large, expensive and full of images with no words – they are not children's picture books!

HAVE A FETISH FOR WATCHES

We love them – maybe it's because a beautifully-designed watch is a joy to look at every second. Like dogs chasing a stick, we'll never tire of it.

BOXES TURN US ON

If we can organise items in boxes, then it's like Christmas, Easter and our Birthday all rolled into one.

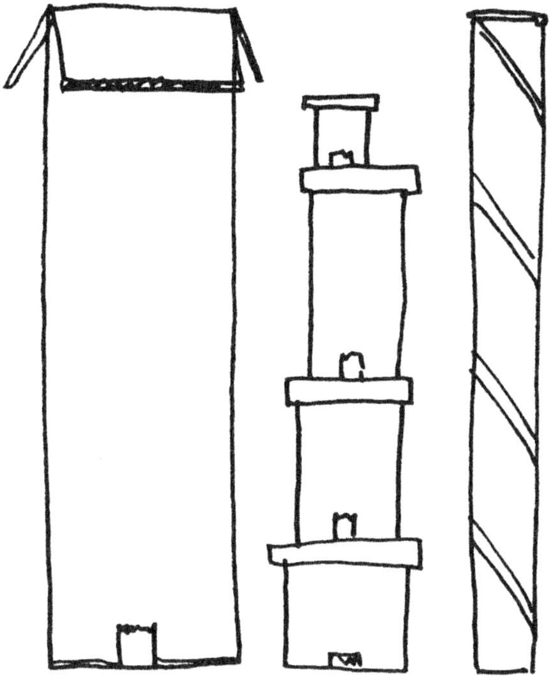

WE REJECT UGLY

It may seem harsh, but designers naturally reject ugly things. This makes it very hard to buy anything to eat, choose a holiday, buy a radio, well, anything. You may just need new bathroom scales, but we can't buy them unless they are beautiful and a feat of design styling. We have a picture of the perfect scales in our head and they must match or no purchase is possible.

WE HATE COMIC SANS

The rest of the world doesn't get designers' hatred of this font. We don't think it's quirky, fun, happy, approachable or easy going. We hate it; it makes our eyes bleed.

BEAUTY IN MUNDANE CRAP

You might look at it and think it's just a water stain on a concrete floor – move on – but designers will see endless possibilities; an idea for a new sports brand logo and complementary app design. It's sad but true!

BRICK

FONTS ARE OUR SPECIALIST SUBJECT

We can talk about typography for hours. Yes, these are the different styles that you can use to change the text in Word. For most people, that's as far as it goes, but definitely not for designers. We can bore you for endless hours and still not be done.

SELECT FONT
ARIAL
COURIER
GEORGIA
GILL SANS
HELVETICA
MINION PRO
MONACO
TIMES
TIMES NEW ROMAN
TREBUCHEN
WINGDINGS

ANYTHING CRAFT IS KING

Beer or coffee – we love anything with ‘craft’ in front of its name. Especially if it’s been made within a ten metre radius of us and costs at least triple its usual price.

C
COFFEE

APPLE PRODUCTS

It's our kryptonite – we love anything Apple. For designers, it's God in physical form; it's like licking royalty on a daily basis.

iSandwich

WE CAN NEVER SLEEP

Famously insomniac, we will lie in bed playing ideas over and over in our heads. Then, in the small hours, we'll frantically scribble notes under the covers, using our iPhones as a torch.

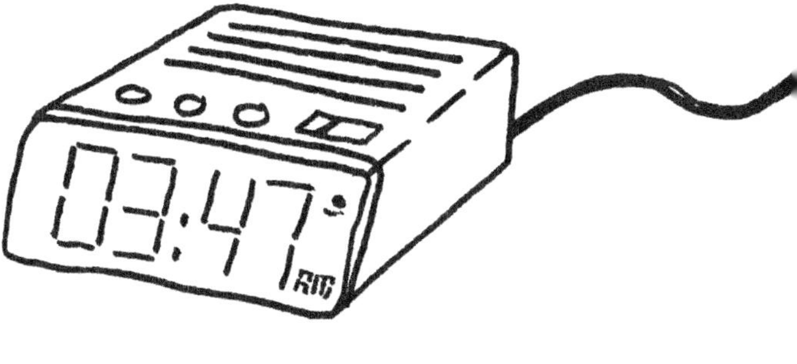
03:47

NOTEBOOK ON US ALWAYS

We may forget to take our keys, wallet or trousers when we leave the house, but we will always have a notebook and pencil with us.

WE CAN NEVER HAVE ENOUGH TOTE BAGS

I'm not sure why, but designers love tote bags – the more unique the better. As if by divine intention, they are the perfect size for an Apple laptop.

WE HATE CABLES

If designers had any political power we would immediately ban cables.

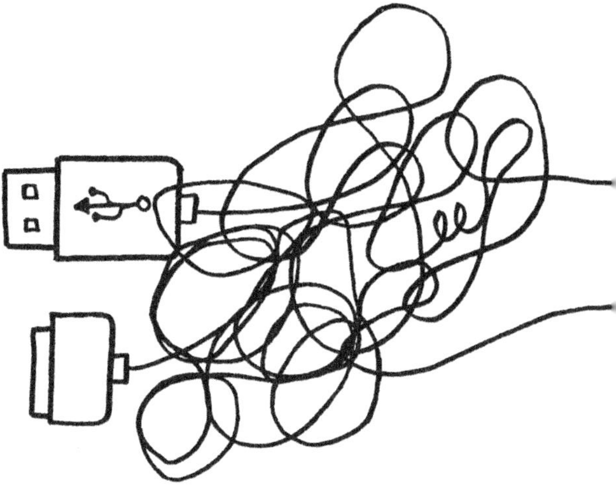

ALWAYS SKETCHING

Those strange drawings we do at moments of instant inspiration. They are to help us get ideas out of our head and onto paper, clearing space for more. But never call them doodles!

BAUHAUS

This is not a goth band but a design school and a kind of church for most designers.

GOOD BRANDING

It makes coffee taste better if the cup has a nice logo and if some shaving foam comes in a lovely handmade box with a matching ribbon, then we must have it!

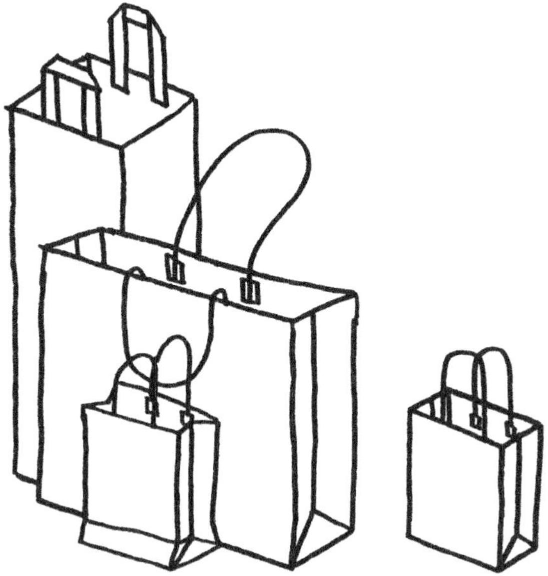

VERY AWARE OF BAD DESIGN

We see it everywhere, but bad design is like someone poking us in the eye with a pencil. Bad logos, awful posters on the tube, terribly typeset menus, the list goes on. We also have to point them out to someone or else we will explode.

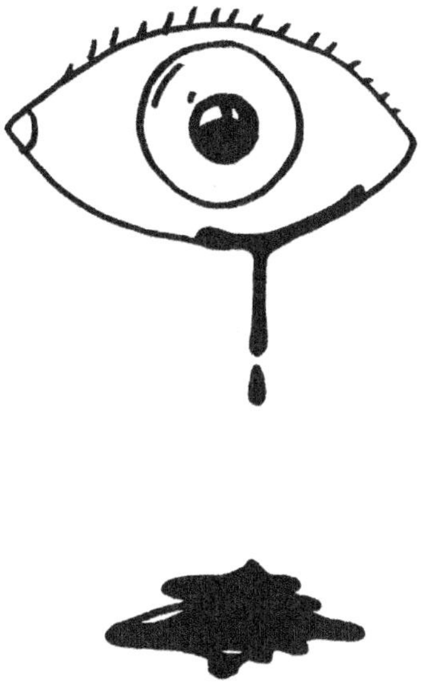

THESE ARE JUST SOME OF THE PAINFUL AND LAUGHABLE FACETS OF LIVING WITH A DESIGNER. THERE ARE MANY MORE, IF YOU HAVE ANY PARTICULAR ONES, WHY NOT EMAIL THEM TO:

QUIRKS@ALANLONG.CO.UK

@SANEANDABLE

Printed in Great Britain
by Amazon

73968602R00041